streets

good food helping good kids

STREETS
RESTAURANT CAFÉ

foreword

by Peter Jon Lindberg,
Editor At Large, Travel + Leisure, New York, New York

I first visited Vietnam in 1997, landing in Saigon on an especially searing late spring afternoon. The heat waves rippling off the tarmac at Tan Son Nhat made the landscape seem mirage-like, and my arrival all the more fantastical. As an American child of the seventies, I'd grown up with images of Vietnam permeating music, movies, and television—from Oliver Stone to Bruce Springsteen, Rambo to Magnum, P.I. Those inherited memories defined my initial encounter in '97. I saw Vietnam's present mostly through the lens of its past. (The past wasn't so far away then: the old U.S. Embassy still stood forlorn on Le Duan Boulevard, and jingling bicycles outnumbered Honda Dream motorbikes.) To have finally arrived myself in this much-storied land—in actual, real-life Vietnam—felt like a minor miracle.

I fell hard for Vietnam on that too-brief visit. It was the beginning of a decades-long obsession with the country, its culture, its language, and its people. I've since returned every year or two, for professional reasons and personal ones—to reconnect with old friends and old haunts. Yet each return might as well be a brand-new encounter, given how quickly Vietnam is evolving. Suddenly another dozen restaurants and boutiques will sprout up like bamboo; gleaming suburbs and resort compounds will claim another rice field or beach. The 27-year-old me would hardly recognize Saigon's skyline today.

It's this continual reinvention—this eternal freshness—that strikes one most in Vietnam. Part of this I attribute to its wondrous cuisine, which of course is synonymous with freshness. Believe me: no matter how many bowls of bun bo Hue you've lustily slurped up; no matter how many market stalls you've combed in search of the perfect cao lau, even your thousandth bite can taste as bright and vivid as your first. This is one of the world's great cuisines, as the rest of the planet is now discovering.

But there's a deeper reason for Vietnam's sense of constant reinvention, and it happens to be the country's greatest resource: its youth. As everyone will remind you, well over half the population is under 35. Young people are the pulsing heart of Vietnamese culture, and it is through them that so many travelers experience the country firsthand. They are the children in school uniforms walking to class through the narrow lanes of Hoi An; the teenage boys playing badminton along the lakeshore in Hanoi; the twentysomethings laughing down Le Loi Street in Saigon; the receptionists at your hotel in Hue, in their silk ao dais. They are the waitstaff, the cooks, the store clerks, the valets and concierges, the motorbike-parkers and souvenir-vendors, the flight attendants and museum guards. They are the astonishingly resourceful and resilient life-force that drives Vietnam's economy forward. Yet too often, too many are locked out of the opportunities such a dynamic economy should provide.

This is where STREETS comes in, with its ingenious and inspired mission: to provide Vietnam's youth with the training, skills, and connections to build lasting, meaningful careers in the restaurant and hotel trades. It is an extraordinary initiative transforming lives in extraordinary ways. Though STREETS is headquartered in Hoi An, the program's reach now extends well beyond Central Vietnam: students in this year's class hail from as far north as Sapa, as far south as a fishing village near Nha Trang. Alumni work in all facets of the food and hospitality industry, across the length of Vietnam and even overseas. (For a look at the very real changes STREETS has brought about, turn to page 21 to read profiles of eight recent graduates.)

I hope the mouthwatering recipes in this book—our most popular dishes from the STREETS Restaurant Café—will inspire delicious adventures in your own kitchen, and that the gorgeous images and moving stories told herein will coax you to visit Vietnam yourself, be it for your first journey or fifteenth. Most of all, I hope you'll consider supporting STREETS, as we continue to grow and to build on these changes, helping even more young people across the country. Thank you for joining us.

acknowledgments

This cookbook, like the STREETS program itself, could not exist without the help and support of so many. Acknowledgments for the book are as much about STREETS and those who work with and support us as they are about the recipes. Perhaps even more so.

First, I want to thank all the young people who have come to STREETS. Whatever they've gained from STREETS, they've given back. They trusted us—and keep in mind that we were foreigners and strangers—enough to come to Hoi An. They lived and learned and worked hard for 18 months. All of our Trainees made a scary-but-brave move, motivated by the desire for a better life, and that in turn has made it possible for those who came after them to have the same opportunity.

My mother was a teacher and my father a lawyer. They were not easy parents, but they were good ones. From my mother I learned about passion for life and teaching. From my father I learned about fairness and decency. They're part of STREETS, too.

Early on we decided that our entire staff, including managers, would have to be Vietnamese. After all, it was their community that we would be working in and serving; their community that we wanted to be part of. The decision had its challenges, especially when it came to communication of two dramatically different mother tongues. But it was the right call, and many of our best friends here in Hoi An are the people that work with us. For their very hard work, especially their commitment to helping disadvantaged Vietnamese youth—not to mention their patience with us—thank you very much. This book is just one part of STREETS that would never have been as good and as authentic if you had not been here.

As you'll see, we have developed a market tour and tasting and now, just recently, a noodle making experience with some of our tour operator partners. They understand what we are about and, as responsible leaders in the travel industry, have worked with us to support our program, even helping to promote and sell this book. Thank you to all the travel companies, especially G Adventures, Insider Journeys and Phoenix Voyages.

We have also been the beneficiaries of much assistance from our many colleagues at New York University and the Institute of Culinary Education in New York City. Our program's standard of excellence is based on the understanding and dedication that NYU and the ICE have for food—cooking and service—and your sharing of your expertise is reflected not only in the recipes in this book but also in our curriculum. Thank you, too, to those of you who covered my teaching responsibilities and the classes I missed while giving me the freedom to go back and forth to Asia as we got STREETS up and running. The list is long, and I can't name every-one here, but I need to give special recognition to Brian Buckley, Andy Gold, Marion Nestle, Ph.D., Ted Siegel, Richard Vajda, Erica Wides and especially Steve Zagor.

Thanks to the ONE Foundation, in Ireland, and Planet Wheeler, in Australia, two of the very generous foundations that supported us and allowed us to get our doors open—and allowed us to complete this book. Your support for STREETS has meant that so many possibilities, which were just that back then, have been realized.

To Tracey Ryan and Peter Cooper of the Ryan Cooper Family Foundation which has helped fund so many classes, programs and Trainees. Your on-going support and friendship are invaluable.

To the many NYC chefs and restaurateurs, already called upon frequently to support so many other good causes, thank you for participating in our annual NYC fund-raising event, which is as critical as anything in supporting what we do. And, to those of you who, as we were putting this book together, took time to answer our many queries about ingredients and methods, thank you again.

STREETS, this book, everything we do would not exist without our board members, who have served and supported us so, so generously with your time, energy, the resources of your respective businesses and your checkbooks, as you signed up for all this and more. Lots of special thanks to our governing board: Phil Baltz, Ruairi Curtin, Jacqueline Lundquist and Rick Smilow .

I would also like to thank our founding board members: Howard Greenstone, William S. Gyves, Mark Maynard-Parisi, Drs. Jennifer Berg and Laurence Simon. You were needed and you responded.

And, certainly, we have to say thank you to the people who helped create this book from the beginning: Lyn Hughes, for her stunning photos and food styling; Matt Wythe, for the beautiful design and layout; Charlie Reed and Amy Morrison, for the writing and editing, especially the story of STREETS and of our featured Trainees. For early help with editing recipes and other valuable suggestions, Ngaire Douglas, as well as the Australian Business Volunteers, much thanks.

But, finally, I admit selfishly, I chose to write these acknowledgements myself, not with the partner who has given more to this program and this book than was ever reasonable to expect of anyone. I did this to be sure that I did not miss the opportunity to say, once again, thank you. Sondra, none of this would ever have been without you.

Thank you, Neal

contents

"Before coming to STREETS my future was very dark, but now I can see and pass all the obstacles in my way. Who would I be if I wasn't lucky and had the chance to be a Trainee at STREETS?

All of my bad feelings have disappeared when I am a Trainee. Now I can make my dream to be the truth, to become a good cook. Nothing can ever show my gratitude to STREETS."

— **Nghe,** STREETS Trainee

Introduction

streets
introduction

Above: Founders Neal Bermas
and Sondra Stewart.

Inspired by the haunting eyes of a small group of impoverished children selling postcards on the sidewalk in Ho Chi Minh City's District 1, STREETS International has taken root as one of Southeast Asia's most innovative social enterprises.

These kids, all around the ages of 9 and 10, were essentially begging for money to buy milk, Neal Bermas, STREETS International founder, recalls of the encounter during his first trip to Vietnam in 1999.

"I wasn't unaccustomed to seeing poverty," says Bermas, then a New York City-based international management consultant, who also taught at New York University and the Institute of Culinary Education. He had traveled extensively and had come across many people living in destitution, in his own country and abroad.

"But those street kids and their sad, dark eyes struck me," says Bermas. "I have carried that image with me ever since."

Over the next several years, Bermas returned frequently to Vietnam and Southeast Asia for business and to explore its exotic terrain, encountering more street children living in desperation. As Vietnam's appeal as an international tourist destination began to grow, so did the concept for STREETS.

"I wanted to do something," says Bermas, who left a comfortable life and successful career in New York to start STREETS in Vietnam.

Bermas saw an opportunity to work with the type of kids he saw living on the streets in poverty, to develop and train them to meet the needs of the country's booming tourism industry. Along with partner Sondra Stewart, a U.S.-based business strategy expert and independent consultant, well-versed in start-up technology companies, he established STREETS International in 2007.

"Our countries share a modern history, both troubling and compelling. Many Americans, like me, grew up with the horrible media images of what the Vietnamese call the 'American War.' To see the relatively rapid evolution between the U.S. and Vietnam to cooperation and friendship called to me."

Despite the tourism dollars flowing into Hoi An and other popular destinations, there is still widespread poverty. Fifty percent of the Vietnamese population lives on less than $2 a day. Unemployment among youth, especially those with a limited education, is remarkably high. There is a reasonably good public education system, but the extremely poor often lack even the small funds required for books and meals at school. Others often go uneducated because of a lack of schools in their area or the need to stay and help at home. These are

> "I wasn't unaccustomed to seeing poverty, but those street kids and their sad, dark eyes struck me. I have carried that image with me ever since. I wanted to do something."
>
> **- Neal Bermas,**
> Founder,
> STREETS International

the disadvantaged, unemployed young people STREETS was established to help.

Some have been victims of human trafficking; their parents duped by promises of room, board and job training for their children, whom they often could not afford to feed. Instead, these false promises ended in forced labor or worse.

"It's unimaginable for most of us to think how a parent could sell their own child," says Bermas. He and Stewart often accompany STREETS staff to conduct the home visit required for each applicant. "I've learned just how difficult and just how desperate life can be. It's heart-breaking."

Above left: Thu Bon River.
Above right: Fresh herbs in the market.

Still, Bermas and Stewart believe that past circumstances, no matter how tragic, should not limit a person's potential. They have developed a rigorous 18-month program based on international culinary and hospitality standards, working closely with friends and colleagues at New York University and the Institute of Culinary Education (ICE) in New York.

STREETS graduates earn a culinary certificate developed in conjunction with ICE, and go on to work in top, five-star hotels, resorts and restaurants in the region. The organization has a 100-percent placement rate.

"It's a comprehensive and tough curriculum, similar to those that you would find in New York, Singapore, London or Melbourne. But, I simply believe if you expect a lot, you get a lot."

- Neal Bermas,
Founder,
STREETS International

"It's a comprehensive and tough curriculum, similar to those that you would find in New York, Singapore, London or Melbourne. But, I simply believe if you expect a lot, you get a lot. People rise to the level they are treated and expected to perform at, whether you're a Wall Street executive or a street kid from Vietnam," Bermas says.

"We have big expectations and high standards. That gives these kids not only the top-notch career skills they need to become self-sufficient, but also the basic human dignity they are entitled to, which is hard to come by when you're in survival mode your whole life."

The Trainees, aged 16 to 22, choose between a culinary track or a professional hospitality track after a six-week orientation. In addition, all participants receive English instruction six days a week, supplemented with intensive tutoring in small groups.

Trainees receive instruction from professional educators in classrooms and a teaching kitchen at the organization's training center. They also spend a minimum of five hours each week practicing their language skills in STREETS' computer lab.

Weekly recreation and life-skills courses teach them everything from how to budget their money and use ATM cards to teambuilding and effective communication. Other subjects include community responsibility, personal hygiene and first-aid.

"House parents" staff the separate boys and girls dormitories and help care for and supervise the kids. Trainees go to the market daily and work together to prepare three nutritious meals for themselves. They receive medical check-ups and healthcare, clothing, uniforms, pedal bikes and a small monthly

Above left: STREETS Trainee.
Above right: The Training Center computer language lab.

Opposite: STREETS Trainee.

allowance. When necessary, STREETS also provides travel costs for students to return home for holidays and emergencies.

After several months of English and career studies, Trainees begin apprenticing with the professional staff and chefs at STREETS Restaurant Café. The restaurant also provides an integral part of the organization's financial sustainability.

"We've spent significant time in developing the model, materials and curriculum for STREETS that we use in Hoi An. We knew this would make it easier to replicate in other areas in Vietnam and around the world," says Stewart. "Our backgrounds are in business, not non-profits. So, we are able to use our experience to create a fiscally sound foundation to allow STREETS to operate as a bona fide social enterprise."

Opposite: STREETS Trainee.

Above left: Temple in the old quarter.
Above right: Characteristic tiled roofs of Hoi An.

Throughout Southeast Asia, the burgeoning tourism industry is changing economies and creating the need for the kind of high-skilled culinary and hospitality professionals STREETS graduates exemplify. Bermas and Stewart plan to expand upon the unique model that is now thriving in Hoi An.

Rated among the top eateries in town, the restaurant serves authentic Vietnamese and international dishes in a contemporary setting. "I don't want anyone coming to eat at STREETS because they feel sorry for the kids," Bermas says. "I want them to come for the excellent food and the superb service."

A registered U.S. 501(c)(3) non-profit based in New York City, STREETS has a board of directors and an advisory panel that boasts internationally renowned chefs, restaurateurs, hospitality professionals and business executives.

"The hospitality and culinary fields now stand out as an area for global career opportunities. Graduates of the STREETS' program not only are well-trained and well-positioned to enter this arena, but to excel in it," says ICE President and CEO Rick Smilow, also a member of the STREETS' board of directors.

"The combination of kitchen, front-of-house and language skills they learn during the 18 months is a potent formula for launching their careers and a lifetime of success."

Bermas, who chairs the board, and Stewart together oversee the program and restaurant in Hoi An. However, they have worked tirelessly to train their all-Vietnamese staff, both at the organization's training headquarters and its restaurant, to run day-to-day operations.

The pair create relationships with the Trainees that strike a warm balance of trust and professionalism. They are family, friends, mentors and employers.

"Providing three meals a day, a clean and safe place to live, exciting and interesting classroom teaching, and lots of respect, decency and hugs, seems to make it work," Bermas says.

Bermas and Stewart chose Hoi An, an ancient trading port to start STREETS because it is at the center of Vietnam's tourism boom. The town was designated an UNESCO 'World Heritage Cultural Site' in 1999 for its well-preserved architecture,

"The combination of kitchen, front-of-house and language skills they learn during the 18 months is a potent formula for launching their careers and a lifetime of success".

– Rick Smilow
President and CEO,
Institute of Culinary Education,
New York, New York

Above left: STREETS Trainee.
Above right: Sidewalk eatery.

which highlights the influence that traders from China, Japan and Europe have had there over the centuries.

Surrounded by lush rice fields, Hoi An's lantern-lit streets, riverside cafes and seemingly endless beaches draw travelers from around the world. While a popular tourist destination, Hoi An remains a village full of old-world charm: men playing Chinese chess in coffee shops, colorful ferry boats docked along the Thu Bon river, tailors who have been plying the family trade for generations, and the common sight of two children on one bike peddling in unison.

"To me, Hoi An, in many ways, is still the real Vietnam," says Bermas, who lives along a quaint alleyway and walks or bikes his way around town most days. He remembers fondly the day STREETS Restaurant Café opened in 2009 in the heart of Hoi An on Le Loi Street to a showering of flowers from nearby neighbors – a customary gesture within the local Vietnamese business community.

"It was so touching to be accepted and welcomed that way," Bermas recalls. "I came here to know and to be part of the Vietnamese community, so that was really special."

The group of desperate kids Bermas met in Ho Chi Minh City more than a decade ago would be about the age of STREETS' inaugural class who graduated in January 2011.

Bermas still remembers their faces clearly, but he and Stewart now delight in watching the profound transformation that occurs in the Trainees' lives. They come in as vulnerable, scared kids and leave confident and well-equipped to start their own careers.

"STREETS provides the skills, security and care they need to develop a career, not just get a job," says Bermas. "Ultimately they define success for themselves and leave with a newfound sense of dignity and hope for their future."

Above right: Hoi An's iconic lanterns.

Market

The Market:
Meet the people and the food of Vietnam

In Vietnam, if you want to get to know the people, a trip to the local market is a must.

A Vietnamese market is a living, breathing entity where travelers can interact with locals and get to know the country's exotic produce, foods and other goods. It's also a place to gain an appreciation of just how much Vietnam's food reflects its culture.

Each year STREETS International connects thousands of tourists eager for a taste of the markets with its Trainee-led culinary tours. The Trainees' passion for the food makes for an inspired excursion. Since a majority of their apprenticing is in the kitchen, these specialty tours were developed, in large part, to give the culinary Trainees an opportunity to interact with guests from around the world. In leading the tours, they practice their English and gain as much from the tours as do the guests.

Typical markets are an informal array of open-air stalls, bustling with vendors, customers and traffic. Goods come in and out mostly on hand carts

Above: Fishmonger at
Tiger Market.

Opposite: Chicken and other meats
for sale at Tiger Market.

and motorbikes, which in Vietnam transport the bulk of goods and are more common than delivery trucks. The markets are a whirlwind of bright colors, pungent aromas and noisy exchanges – a sight to behold, more intriguing than many museums and historic sites.

Hordes of suppliers and vendors convene at dawn everyday at markets throughout the country, from rural villages to small neighborhoods to large cities. Visiting one is a sensory experience of exotic sights, sounds and smells. Shoppers inspect the produce, ask for special cuts of meat and haggle with fishmongers.

Vendors are usually friendly and always eager to make a sale. Everything is displayed on ramshackle tables or on the ground in colorful plastic baskets, tended by women squatting next to them in typical Vietnamese fashion. Noodles are cut using hand-cranked machines and piled in nest-like bundles. There are no shopping carts, and transactions are made in cash; no registers, no receipts, no returns.

The organized chaos is exhilarating but can also be intimidating for those more accustomed to sterile supermarkets full of pre-packaged, processed foods.

STREETS tours navigate through the confusion. The tours start and end at the STREETS Restaurant Café on Le Loi street in the heart of Hoi An. The local Tan An Market was chosen since it offers a more authentic experience than the popular riverside market in the center of the town.

Guests are introduced to a variety of rice papers and rice noodles, the ubiquitous nuoc mam fermented fish sauce, dragon fruit, bitter melon,

pomelo and Vietnamese basil and mint. These are among the the most common ingredients used in Vietnamese cuisine and the inspired dishes served at STREETS Restaurant Café.

Upon seeing the fuchsia-colored skin of the rambutan fruit, protruding with pliable spikes, encasing a white flesh with the texture of a grape, an Australian tour guest exclaimed: "They look like hairy, pink golf balls!"

Later, at the tasting, which is part of the tour, she was shown how to peel a rambutan. "This is delicious," she said. "My new favorite fruit!"

Opposite: Making rice noodles at
Tiger Market.

Top left: Rambutan.
Right: Dragon fruit.
Bottom left: Nuoc mam (fish sauce).

15

> "Learning how green papayas and mangos are commonly used here and how to distinguish all the fresh herbs is really helpful. Now that I know what all these things are, I can't wait to cook some Vietnamese dishes."
> — STREETS Market Tour guest

A British guest said he was eager to go to the Asian market when he got back home, thanks to the STREETS market tour.

"Learning how green papayas and mangos are commonly used here and how to distinguish all the fresh herbs is really helpful," he said, smiling while jotting notes and taking photos. "Now that I know what all these things are, I can't wait to cook some Vietnamese dishes."

The markets are a frenzied and beautiful tableau, anchored largely by women. In Vietnam, women are generally responsible for food shopping and also dominate the markets – tending stalls, negotiating deals, scaling fish, butchering meat and displaying produce. Men typically are busy fishing, farming and tending to livestock.

The lack of widespread refrigeration in Vietnam means the food must always be fresh. The Vietnamese go to the market at least once, if not twice, each day. This keeps the markets constantly busy. Produce, meat, poultry and seafood – mostly from local sources – are delivered and sold throughout the day. Refrigerators are becoming more common, but many Vietnamese households function without one. Either way, markets are essential to the Vietnamese way of life.

During the tours at the Tan An Market, also called the Tiger Market because of the nearby Tiger Temple, Trainees explain how little goes to waste in Vietnam, least of all the food. The Vietnamese cleverly consume every part of the animal, fish and produce. While things such as chicken feet and sweet potato leaves likely would be discarded in western kitchens, such items are cooked in Vietnam in ingenious and delicious ways.

The culinary Trainees engage guests not only with explanations about the food, its preparation and how it's eaten in Vietnam, but also with anecdotes about the role food plays in ancestor-worship ceremonies. A majority of the country is Buddhist, and most homes and businesses have a shrine where offerings of prepared food and fruits are presented often, if not daily.

Above left: STREETS Trainee
leading tour.
Above right: Tiger Temple.

Opposite: Fresh vegetable for sale
at Tiger Market.

The STREETS market tours include a stop at the funerary stand, found in any Vietnamese market. These stands sell incense, paper clothes, paper cell phones and fake money to be burned in ceremonies to honor their ancestors and deceased family members. Many believe the symbolic items are used by the dead in the afterlife. An "An gio" meal is another common ritual, that honors a deceased family member by cooking their favorite foods on the anniversary of their death.

At the end of each day, all of the produce, meats, poultry and seafood are packed up, and the vendors disband as quickly as they set up at daybreak. It's a fascinating event that takes place everyday, and any trip to Vietnam would be incomplete without a visit to the market. Diverse yet basic, disorganized but functional, frenetic and friendly, the markets, perhaps more than any other single aspect of the country's culture, typify daily life in Vietnam.

Opposite: Grilling rice paper.

Above left: Star fruit.
Above right: STREETS Trainee leading tour.

Profiles

Lê Thị Thu Sương

Age: 20
Position: Server, La Maison 1888, Intercontinental Da Nang Sun Peninsula Resort
Home: Dien Hong Commune, Dien Ban District, Quang Nam Province

Abandoned by her mother, Suong grew up with her grandparents in Quang Nam Province's rural Dien Ban district, about 10 miles (16 kilometers) northwest of Hoi An.

A smart girl who always liked to read, she graduated from high school and longed to go to college. But her grandparents, aging subsistence rice farmers, struggled just to feed themselves. They could not afford to provide their granddaughter with the luxury of a college education.

Suong was forced to take the first job she could find. At 18, she began working in a shoe factory, a "sweat shop" environment, where she labored long hours for little money.

After five months of working for almost nothing, she applied to STREETS International after hearing about the program from a friend. Without a phone and desperate for the opportunities she knew STREETS presented, Suong often biked from her village to Hoi An to check the status of her application – a three-hour trek.

"I was very eager," Suong remembers. "I didn't want to stop my education after high school. But my grandparents have no money." She wanted to learn English and work in the bustling tourism hub, a world away from her poor, rural farming community.

It was a dream STREETS helped Suong realize. Upon graduating, she agreed to help the program and stay on during the busy tourist season as a server.

Suong honed her newly acquired hospitality skills and English at the restaurant. She worked there for nine months and went on to get a job at the Intercontinental Da Nang Sun Peninsula Resort, one of the most luxurious hotels in the region. Not only is Suong thriving there, she was also promoted to a team leader to help train and supervise others.

On her days off, she brings food, milk and other basic necessities to her grandparents. They discourage their granddaughter from frivolous spending with her newfound income – more than double the average monthly salary in Vietnam.

Their meager home still houses Suong's small but jam-packed bookcase, a testament to her life-long desire for learning. She still thinks about continuing to study English and perhaps even applying to university.

"I want to continue my education," Suong says, a flash of determination washing over her bright eyes. "STREETS changed my life a lot. I can speak English now. I can study now. I owe a big 'thank you' to Miss Sondra and Mr. Neal."

Suong says she hopes visitors to Vietnam and to STREETS Restaurant Café will enjoy learning about the country's rich culture and delicious cuisine. "If they can remember the food, they can remember the people."

Cao Thị Hồng Vân

Age: 22
Position: Room Service Order Taker and Server, Hyatt Regency Da Nang Resort and Spa
Home: Tan Chinh Commune, Thanh Khe District, Da Nang City

Van's mother died when she was just 15. Her mother was a pharmacist and the family's main source of income. Van's father soon abandoned her and her younger sister. The girls were forced to live with an aunt and uncle, who could provide little more than basic shelter.

"I did not have anything. I only had myself."

At 19, Van was unemployed and desperate to find a way to support herself and her sister when she heard about STREETS International. She needed what they offered; food, a safe place to live and career training for kids with nowhere to turn.

The Da Nang native had never been away from the difficult conditions of her home before moving to STREETS in Hoi An about 19 miles (30 kilometers) to the south. "When I arrived I was scared of everything," Van says. "But everybody was really kind to me and I felt very welcome."

After a few months, her fellow Trainees and the staff at STREETS began to feel like family. "We live together. We eat together. We learn together."

Van says she realized how close the bond was when she and some of the other girls contracted dengue fever and were hospitalized for a week. The entire organization helped the sick girls, especially the nurturing "house parents" who live in the STREETS girls and boys dormitories to supervise and care for the kids.

"I can't describe the feeling," she says of the experience. "Everyone helped us so much. We all take care of each other."

Just two weeks after graduating from STREETS, Van was hired by the Hyatt Regency. She quickly demonstrated her strong command of English and hospitality skills and was placed in the vital room service department.

The professionalism and enthusiasm she learned at STREETS did not go unnoticed by the Hyatt. In 2012, Van was named 'employee of the year,' winning an all-expense paid vacation to Singapore.

"I never believed I would go to a place like Singapore, or even leave Da Nang. Now I want to travel," she says, beaming.

Van says she appreciated the work ethic impressed upon her at STREETS.

"I want to do everything until it's complete and perfect," she says. "I have passion to do my job and I learned this from STREETS."

She is now able to help support her family and pay for her sister to attend nursing school. She is also saving to build a tomb for her mother, who she says "always protects me."

"I am so lucky because I found STREETS," she says. "Now I want to help other people, too."

Kỳ Xuân Núi

Age: 24
Position: Server, STREETS Restaurant Café
Home: Ka Dang Commune, Dong Giang District, Quang Nam Province

Nui had never seen anyone from outside his rural mountain community until he was 15. He and his friend hiked two hours up a mountain one day to catch a glimpse of the pale-skinned American they heard was volunteering in their remote part of the world.

"At that time I didn't think it's possible for me to work with foreigners," he remembers thinking. "I could not communicate with them."

Nui is Catu, an ethnic minority group of Vietnam who reside mainly in the Truong Son Mountains about 60 miles (95 kilometers) west of Hoi An. His village is isolated with limited access, especially when its roads wash out in the rainy season.

Many Catu live off the land in villages considered primitive even by Vietnamese standards. Such communities are dwindling as the younger generation increasingly migrates to cities in hope of finding jobs.

Nui and several family members were lucky enough to receive money from an NGO to attend a high school several hours away in Dai Loc.

After high school, he made the long trip south to Ho Chi Minh City to get a job at a meat-processing factory, where he worked in deplorable conditions for low wages. Eventually, he moved closer to home. He found a job in Da Nang at a mechanic shop, working for room and board.

Although he got out of his village, life wasn't getting much better. He heard about STREETS and "knew this was a chance for me." Nui was overjoyed when he was accepted into the program.

Bustling with tourists and touts, motorbikes and bicycles, Hoi An overwhelmed him when he first arrived.

"It was a bit scary and a little strange," he says. Nui grew up speaking the Catu language. Not only did he have to learn English, but as with other ethnic minority kids at STREETS, he also had to learn to read and write Vietnamese. "Now I can go anywhere," he says. "I don't worry."

After graduating, Nui was selected to work as a server at STREETS Restaurant Café, a track some graduates are offered to help maintain the consistent quality of the restaurant. "I like my job. When the guests smile and they enjoy their meal, I feel happy."

He spends his day off each week at the STREETS Training Center. He uses the computer language lab to continue studying English and to search online for future job prospects.

The boy whose first contact with the outside world was as a teenager, now aspires to travel and work abroad. His eyes flashing with excitement at the prospect; he dreams of working in a five-star resort in Dubai.

"Without STREETS I would end up back in my village as a farmer, and life would be very difficult" Nui says. "Now I know I can have a better life."

Giàng Thị Sáng

Age: 18
Position: Cook, STREETS Restaurant Café
Home: Lao Chai Village, Sapa District, Lao Cai Province

After graduating from STREETS in Hoi An, Sang Thi Giang journeyed home to Sapa a different girl.

"I am so fat and so white that my family didn't recognize me," Sang says with a laugh, recalling her first visit home. Her village is roughly 785 miles (1,260 kilometers) from Hoi An in the mountainous region of northwest Vietnam.

In her culture, "fat" and "white" aren't insults. They signify that she now has enough to eat and no longer labors in the sun, unlike many H'mong people in Lao Cai Province.

While the men and boys toil in the fields, the women and girls trek from their outlying villages into Sapa city to sell their handicrafts to tourists. Sang and her mother hiked for hours to make the four-mile trek (seven kilometers) every day to sell their handmade tapestries, characteristic of the region.

School was never an option for Sang, whose family needed her to contribute to the household income. Sang's family, like others, could not spare the manpower nor afford to buy schoolbooks and meals. Despite their efforts, many of the working children in Sapa often go hungry. Sang and her eight brothers and sisters were no exception.

Sang educated herself, picking up English words and phrases from the tourists she sold to, who were charmed by the graceful and smart young girl.

At 16, Sang gained sponsorship to a local English center for H'mong children, the place where she learned about STREETS. She was ecstatic upon being accepted but her family disapproved. They needed her to stay and help sell the family's wares.

"My mother didn't want me to leave Sapa" Sang recalls. But the tenacious teenager finally persuaded her family to agree.

She excelled during the 18-month culinary program and after graduating she was hired as a cook at STREETS Restaurant Café.

Sang now sends part of her income back home. Her family has gained a newfound respect for the ambitious young woman.

"My mother cried and told me she is proud of me. She told me she was sorry for not trusting me about going to STREETS," Sang says. "I told her, 'Mother, that was the past, let us focus on the future.'"

She is thriving but still misses her family. She plans to eventually move back to Sapa to work in one of the growing number of resorts there.

For now, she is focused on her career and enjoys her independence. But she looks forward to going home, where she hopes to pass on the life-changing skills she acquired to other kids.

Trần Thị Châu Phương

Age: 23
Position: Server and Bartender, The Nam Hai
Home: Tan Hiep Commune, Cham Islands, Quang Nam Province

Phuong was born full of passion.

"My mother said I have fire in my body," Phuong declares with a sparkle in her eye.

But until she came to STREETS at the age of 19, she had little to be energized about.

She grew up on the Cham Islands, eight islets about 12 miles (20 kilometers) east of Hoi An in the South China Sea. It's a popular destination for day-trippers and scuba divers visiting Hoi An, but the people of the Cham Islands struggle. The locals benefit little from the seasonal influx of tourists. There is no running water, healthcare or high school. Many families, like Phuong's, rely on subsistence fishing – a difficult and often dangerous existence.

Phuong was fortunate to leave the isolated island and live with a distant relative so she could attend high school in Hoi An. She remembers enjoying sporadic encounters with foreigners and dreaming of finding work in the tourism industry.

Even after being accepted into the STREETS program, Phuong was hesitant about the opportunity. "They give us food, and bikes, a place to live and money," she says. "But I wonder, what do they want from us?"

She had never experienced such generosity, including medical care to diagnose and treat her thyroid condition.

Phuong had trouble adjusting to the rigorous schedule and structure at STREETS. In addition to hospitality and culinary training, the program is designed to teach Trainees basic life skills, including hygiene, personal responsibility, communication, teamwork and career development skills.

With time, Phuong learned more than the hospitality skills she needed for a career. She developed the interpersonal skills everyone needs for a good life. "At STREETS, we learn life skills, like how to speak with colleagues. I know how to control myself, and this is good for your job."

She is now able to help colleagues settle disputes and handle customer complaints with professional ease.

After graduating from STREETS, Phuong was hired as a server at The Nam Hai, an award-winning, five-star resort on a private beach outside of Hoi An.

Now, she helps support her struggling parents and relatives on the Cham Islands with basic necessities. She also helps mentor recent STREETS graduates as they begin to start their own careers.

"I'm so lucky to have STREETS and to have a family. It makes me hurt because I know there are some people who have it more difficult than me," she says. "It is my dream to help people."

Hồ Ngọc Diệu

Age: 24
Position: Commis Chef III and Cooking Class Instructor, Anantara Hoi An Resort
Home: Thuy Xuan Commune, Hue City, Thua Thien Hue Province

Dieu grew up in an orphanage in Hue, the ancient imperial capital three hours north of Hoi An. His father died in a flood. His mother, unable to care for her son, abandoned him.

The orphanage provided shelter and schooling, but Dieu was alone. In spite of these circumstances, he developed his creative side, painting landscapes and portraits on scrap paper. He also taught himself to play the traditional bamboo flute when he was a boy.

While living at the orphanage, Dieu participated in an English outreach program run by STREETS. He attended the two-hour English class six days a week. His hard work and smile were noted, and he was accepted into the organization's training program in Hoi An.

Leaving Hue, the only place he had ever known, was not easy. Nevertheless, he envisioned a better life and a brighter future.

When he came to STREETS, Dieu not only escaped poverty, he blossomed. As he studied English and trained to be a cook, he transitioned from a shy boy into a competent and professional young man.

"STREETS changed me a lot," he says. "I am confident now. Learning English was the most important thing for me."

After graduating from STREETS, Dieu was hired as a cook at the luxury Anantara Hoi An Resort.

His artistic ability helps him with his work in the kitchen. Dieu uses Vietnam's fruits, vegetables and herbs as a palette of colors, flavors and aromas when preparing the many delicious dishes on the resort's menu.

The hotel's executive chef and general manager recognized his talent. They saw that he had top-notch culinary skills, a winning personality and a good command of English. They selected him to teach guests at the resort's daily cooking classes. This high-profile position is rarely afforded to such a young chef.

Guests in his cooking class would likely find it hard to believe that the well-spoken, handsome young man was ever a shy orphan who sometimes didn't have enough to eat.

"I love to see the guests happy," he says, with an infectious smile that charms most anyone he meets. "It makes me feel good, like I have done a good job."

Nguyễn Xuân Đô

Age: 25
Position: Executive Chef, The Rachel, Da Nang
Home: Tan Hiep Commune, Cham Islands, Quang Nam Province

Born on the isolated Cham Islands, Do became an orphan at 12 when his father died and his mother abandoned him at his grandfather's house in rural Quang Nam Province.

Three years later he was left at an orphanage in Hoi An. He would live there until he was 18.

At the orphanage, Do was tasked with helping prepare meals. It was basic, but his innate culinary abilities began to show. Do caught the attention of the center's Australian director, who later introduced him to STREETS.

He spoke only a few words of English when he came to the program. "But at STREETS we must speak English everywhere," Do says. "Mr. Neal wants us to even dream in English."

He thrived in his culinary studies. The kitchen was an exciting place and became a second home.

"I liked to attend class and go to the restaurant," he says. "In the kitchen, there is so much action. You are not bored in that life."

Do not only was dreaming in English, he was dreaming big. Just two weeks after graduating he was hired as a commis chef at The Nam Hai, the renowned five-star beach resort outside of Hoi An.

He worked at the resort for a year and a half, earning three promotions and being named 'employee of the quarter.' He was a rising star at The Nam Hai when he was offered his dream job as the executive chef at The Rachel, a prominent, new restaurant along the Han River in downtown Da Nang.

"I wanted to try something new. I wanted to design a menu," says Do, who at the age of 23, jumped from a beginning chef to managing a kitchen and a staff. Although the experience has been challenging, Do has risen to the occasion thanks to the sense of confidence and experience he gained through STREETS.

STREETS founder Neal Bermas is "tough," Do says. "He holds all the Trainees to a high standard." Do adopted his mentor's expectations for his own staff at The Rachel.

"I believe in myself, believe in my knowledge and believe in my job. I'm very thankful to Mr. Neal. He gave me wings," Do says. "I can do anything because I always believe in myself and trust myself now because STREETS believed in me and taught me."

"I think I am very lucky," he continues. "If I did not come to STREETS I would not be successful. I would not know how to fly." Now that he's airborne, the sky is the limit. "My dream is to open my own restaurant one day."

Lê Đức Phấn

Age: 22
Position: Commis Chef, La Maison 1888, Intercontinental Da Nang Sun Peninsula Resort
Home: Phuoc Thai Commune, Hoa Vang District, Da Nang City

Phan began cooking at the age of seven. He started by boiling rice in a rusty tin can over an open fire, just like he'd seen his mother do. He took over this responsibility so his parents could work the fields. His first batch of rice burned. But Phan quickly perfected this rudimentary cooking technique used by poor families in rural villages throughout Vietnam.

"I learn from looking," Phan says. "After that I cook everyday for my family."

As he got older, he learned to kill and cook the occasional chicken his family could afford to buy.

Phan grew up extremely poor in the outskirts of Da Nang, about 30 miles (48 kilometers) northwest of Hoi An. He was raised on land contaminated by dioxin during what the Vietnamese refer to as the 'American War.' It was designated as an "Agent Orange affected area" by the Vietnamese government, which provides assistance to residents still suffering from exposure to the poison. A local NGO helped fund his and his twin brother's high school education.

When he was accepted at STREETS at age 19, Phan says he never thought he would be lucky enough to have such an opportunity come his way.

He found the rigorous training program difficult. Picking up culinary skills was a challenge that he was not sure he could master.

With lots of practice and tutoring from the STREETS staff, Phan eventually excelled in the same knife skills he once struggled with. "I push myself to go on. STREETS taught me how to do that," he says. Professional knife skills are requisite for cooking at any fine-dining establishment, and Phan's mastery of them eventually paid off.

After graduating, he worked for a month at a local restaurant in Hoi An. He then interviewed for a job at the Intercontinental Da Nang Sun Peninsula Resort, one of the region's most prestigious hotels. Phan was specially selected for a position as a commis chef to work under the country's only three-star Michelin rated chef at the hotel's La Maison 1888.

From cooking rice in a can to preparing French cuisine with a world-renowned chef, Phan overcame the odds.

Along with a personal sense of success and a newfound ability to provide for himself, he also has enough money to help support his parents and unemployed twin brother.

"STREETS changed my life a lot and now I can help my family," says the soft-spoken young man. When asked about the most valuable thing he learned, Phan replies: "I do everything with my heart, not for the money."

Recipes
from the restaurant

Fresh Summer Rolls
Gỏi cuốn

Rice paper rolls are a Vietnamese speciality. Authentic rolls are prepared with fresh rice paper made from a rice flour batter. The batter is quickly spread thinly and evenly across a taut, cotton covering (like cheese cloth) over a pot of boiling water. When a ladle of batter has been spread, a lid is held firmly over the pot to steam it. When the mixture is set, the rice paper is gently lifted from the cloth using a long, narrow stick. Substitute store-bought rice paper to replicate this quintessential Vietnamese dish. Serves four.

ingredients

rice paper sheets, 20 pieces

pork, cooked and thinly sliced, 7 oz/200 g

shrimp, cooked, peeled, sliced horizontally, 7 oz/200 g

pickled carrot and radish, 3½ oz/100 g

cabbage, finely shredded and pickled, 3½ oz/100 g

lettuce leaves, 20 all but four roughly shredded

julienned carrot and green papaya, 3 tablespoons

Vietnamese sweet and sour fish sauce

nuoc mam (fish sauce), ¼ cup

sugar, ½ cup

fresh-squeezed lemon juice, ½ cup

garlic, 2 cloves, minced

red chilis, 2, minced

Toss together pork and pickled carrot, radish and cabbage. Quickly dip dry rice paper sheet in wide bowl of warm water. Shake off excess liquid and place sheet on dinner plate or other smooth surface to assemble the rolls. Lay some shredded lettuce on one piece of rice paper between the center of the rice paper and closest edge. Top with 1.5 tablespoons of pork mixture. Lay two shrimp halves on top of filling. Fold in closest edge, tucking it firmly around filling. Fold in other two sides and then roll firmly. These rolls can also be left open at one end if desired. Garnish with lettuce leaf and julienned carrot and papaya. Accompany with a dipping bowl of Vietnamese sweet and sour fish sauce.

Crispy Spring Rolls
Nem Rán

This deep-fried roll differs from the salad-like summer roll. It's made with a basket-weave rice paper, unique to central Vietnam. When fried, this special rice paper becomes especially delicate and crispy. This recipe yields about 20 rolls. Serves four.

ingredients

rice paper, 20 sheets
garlic, finely chopped, 4 large cloves
shallot, finely chopped, 1½ tablespoons
pork, minced, 7 oz/200 g
wood ear mushrooms, soaked, finely sliced, 4 tablespoons
taro, boiled and mashed, 4 tablespoons
carrot, finely grated, 4 tablespoons
celery, finely chopped, 1½ tablespoons
salt and pepper to taste
fresh herbs, such as mint and basil
lettuce leaves

Vietnamese sweet and sour fish sauce
nuoc mam (fish sauce), ¼ cup
sugar, ½ cup
fresh-squeezed lemon juice, ½ cup
garlic, 2 cloves, minced
red chilis, 2, minced

Use a food processor to grind garlic and shallots to a paste, add pork, mushroom, taro, carrot, celery, salt and pepper and mix well. Place one tablespoon of filling onto rice paper between center and closest edge. Fold rice paper tightly over filling then fold in each side firmly. Proceed to roll up, keeping filling compact. Repeat with remaining filling. Deep fry a few rolls at a time quickly in hot oil. Drain on paper towel before arranging on plate. Decorate with fresh herbs and lettuce leaves. Serve with Vietnamese sweet and sour fish sauce.

White Rose Dumplings
Bánh Bông Hồng Trắng

A signature dish of Hoi An, the traditional White Rose Dumpling gets its name from its shape. The recipe is more than 120 years old and reflects Hoi An's Chinese community of the 17th century with its dim sum-like quality. Descendants of the family who originated this delicacy still produce it today. While the exact shape may be elusive when trying to re-create at home, the dumpling ideally should resemble a rose, its petals formed by the folded edges of the rice paper. If fresh rice skins are not available, use commercial rice paper softened by soaking in water. Serves four.

ingredients

rice paper skins, 20 pieces
raw shrimp, peeled 16 oz/500 g
garlic, minced, 2 teaspoons
shallot, minced, 2 teaspoons
salt, 1 teaspoon
pepper, 1 teaspoon
sesame oil, 1 teaspoon

sweet fish dipping sauce
nuoc mam (fish sauce), 1 cup
sugar, 1½ cups
water, 3 cups

Put shrimp, garlic, shallots, salt and pepper and sesame oil in a food processor, mix well. Put damp rice paper wrapper in palm of hand, place one teaspoon of mixture in center and fold in corners to form the shape of a flower. Steam for five minutes. Serve with sweet fish dipping sauce.

Spicy Chicken Wings
Cánh Gà Nướng

 Grilled chicken wings are a favorite among the Vietnamese. Most all parts of a chicken make it to the grill at local barbecue stands where grilled chicken feet are a particular treat. The Vietnamese often enjoy their wings with beer, which typically is served in small glasses over ice. Serves four.

ingredients

chicken wings, 8, cut in half at joint, 16 pieces
lemongrass, chopped, 6 tablespoons
garlic, 6 large cloves chopped
shallots, chopped, 3 tablespoons
chili sauce, 3 tablespoons
bbq sauce, any commercial brand, 2 tablespoons
soy sauce, 8 tablespoons
honey, 3 tablespoons

chili mayonnaise dipping sauce

mayonnaise, 4 tablespoons
lemon juice, ½ teaspoon
Hoi An chili sauce, 2 teaspoons

Combine lemongrass, garlic and shallots in a food processor to make a paste. Add chili, bbq and soy sauces plus honey. Place chicken wings in marinade for at least 30 minutes. Grill until well-cooked.

The thick, jam-like Hoi An chili sauce used in this dipping sauce is a specialty of the ancient town. Substitute with commonly available Thai-style hot sauce (such as Sriracha) and Thai sweet chili sauce (such as Mae Ploy.) Add gradually to mayonnaise, checking for taste. Serve sauce with wings.

Crispy Calamari Rings
Mực Chiên Xù

This recipe was a winning entry in the STREETS "Trainee Cooking Contest," an event that was introduced during the inaugural class. The cooking contest is held with each class of Trainees as they near the end of their orientation in the 18-month program. The contest aims to inspire both the Trainees and the menu at STREETS Restaurant Café. This dish is simple but noteworthy for its clean taste and use of fresh, local squid. Serves four.

ingredients

calamari rings cut from squid hood, 16 oz oz/500 g
salt and pepper to taste
chili sauce, 3 tablespoons
all-purpose flour, 1 cup
eggs, 2
breadcrumbs, 1 cup
lettuce leaves, 4
carrot and green papaya, shredded, 3 tablespoons

wasabi mayonnaise

mayonnaise, 1 cup
wasabi, 1 tablespoon
spring onions, 2 tablespoons, used to garnish

Marinate calamari with salt, pepper and chili sauce. Dip calamari rings in flour, lightly beaten egg and then breadcrumbs. Placing the flour and breadcrumbs in separate plastic or paper bags makes for cleaner and easier coating. Heat oil until slight smoke is visible. Deep fry in small batches until crisp. Add wasabi gradually to mayonnaise, checking for taste, to make dipping sauce. Drain calamari rings on kitchen paper, arrange on plate and serve with bowl of wasabi mayonnaise. Garnish with lettuce leaf and shredded carrot and papaya.

Papaya Salad with Dried Beef
Gỏi Đu Đủ trộn Bò Khô

What makes this common Vietnamese salad unique to westerners is its use of unripened, green papayas. Although the tropical fruit is best known when it's ripe and sweet, green papayas add a crisp and tart element that make wonderful salads. Vietnamese also often cut green papayas in wedges and dip them in a dry concoction of salt, pepper and chili. The dried beef used in this recipe at STREETS Restaurant Café is a shredded jerky-like meat that is sweet, salty and slightly spicy. Serves four.

ingredients

green papaya, julienned, 1½ cups

carrot, julienned, ¾ cup

onion, finely sliced, ½ cup

dried beef, 6 oz/185 g

shallot oil, 4 tablespoons (fry chopped shallots in oil until brown then remove shallots)

fried shallots, 4 tablespoons

peanuts, dry roasted, 4 tablespoons

lettuce leaves, 12

mint leaves, ½ cup

prawn crackers, 2-4 per serving

Vietnamese sweet and sour fish sauce

nuoc mam (fish sauce), ¼ cup

sugar, ½ cup

fresh-squeezed lemon juice, ½ cup

garlic, 2 cloves, minced

red chilis, 2, minced

In a large bowl toss together papaya, carrot, onion and dried beef. Add shallot oil and Vietnamese sweet and sour fish sauce. Mix gently. To serve, pile onto plate, scatter with fried shallots and peanuts. Garnish with lettuce, mint leaves and prawn crackers.

Mango Chicken Salad
Gỏi Xoài trộn Gà

This is a simple, refreshing salad that calls for small, unripened (green) Vietnamese mangos. As with the unripened papaya, they are a little bitter, but great for salads. When preparing at home, substitute any green mango available to retain the tartness this salad intends to deliver. Serves four.

ingredients

chicken breast, 320 g
bbq sauce, any commercial brand, 8 tablespoons
fresh green mango, peeled and cubed, 11 oz/345 g
lettuce leaves

passion fruit dressing

mayonnaise, 1 cup
sugar, 2 tablespoons
salt, 2 teaspoons
passion fruit juice, 8 tablespoons
chili sauce, 1 tablespoon

Marinate chicken breast in bbq sauce for 15 minutes. Grill until well-cooked. Allow to cool, then dice the same size as mango cubes. Mix passion fruit dressing ingredients, then fold into chicken and mango mixture. Serve on a bed of lettuce leaves.

Pomelo Salad with Shrimp
Gỏi Bưởi trộn Tôm

Pomelo is the star of this salad. Akin to grapefruit, pomelo is less acidic, with a meatier and whiter flesh. It's a hard fruit to peel and requires a sharp knife, but it's well worth the effort. The salad is best when dressed just before serving. Serves four.

ingredients

pomelo, 1 (substitute with 2 grapefruits)
shrimp, cooked, peeled & halved horizontally, 13 oz/400 g
onion, julienned strips, 6 oz/185 g
carrot, julienned, 6 oz/185 g
fresh mint leaves, ¼ cup
crushed peanuts, 4 tablespoons
fried shallots, 4 tablespoons
lettuce leaves, 12
red chili, finely sliced, 2

Vietnamese sweet and sour fish sauce

nuoc mam (fish sauce), ¼ cup
sugar, ½ cup
fresh-squeezed lemon juice, ½ cup
garlic, 2 cloves, minced
red chilis, 2, minced

Peel the pomelo with sharp knife, removing all pith. If grapefruit is used, increase the amount of sugar to tone down its acidity. Split pomelo into segments, making sure all membrane is removed. Slice into bite-size pieces. In large bowl, toss together pomelo, shrimp, onion, carrot, mint, peanuts and fried shallots. Stir in Vietnamese sweet and sour fish sauce. Plate with lettuce leaves and chili slices.

Squid Salad with Tamarind Sauce
Gỏi Mực sốt me

STREETS Restaurant Café buys fresh squid daily at the local fish market for this dish, and recommends using only fresh squid when preparing it at home. This dish is characterized by the use of tamarind paste, which adds sweet and sour elements that combine well with squid. Tamarind is a small, brown pod that grows on trees. It is typically sold in paste form by the jar. However, STREETS makes its own tamarind paste, which when cooked fills the restaurant with a delightfully pungent aroma. Serves four.

ingredients

squid, 1½ lb/750 g
fresh mint leaves, ¼ cup
celery, julienned, ½ cup
carrot, julienned, ¾ cup
onion, finely sliced, ¾ cup
ginger, julienned, ¼ cup
oil, 1 tablespoon
lettuce leaves, 12
fried shallots, 4 tablespoons
peanuts, chopped, 4 tablespoons
chili, finely sliced, 2

tamarind sauce

tamarind paste, 5 tablespoons
ginger, finely sliced, 1 tablespoon
garlic, finely chopped 1 tablespoon
chili, finely sliced, ½ tablespoon
fish sauce, 2 tablespoons
sugar, 2 tablespoons
salt, ½ teaspoon
oil, 1 tablespoon

Clean fresh whole squid, then put in saucepan and cover with water. Bring to boil, cooking lightly until done. Rinse and cut into bite size pieces. (Fresh, prepared squid hoods are boiled until white.) Allow to cool.

In large bowl, toss together squid, mint, celery, carrot, onion, ginger and oil. For tamarind sauce: Sauté garlic and ginger and mix together with other sauce ingredients. Blend in mayonnaise and oil. Stir sauce through salad. Serve piled onto plate, garnished with lettuce and topped with fried shallots, peanuts and sliced chili.

Vietnamese Tomato and Cucumber Salad

Xà Lách Dầu Giấm

This salad typifies the use of simple ingredients and fresh produce that are available year-round in Vietnam, which is not always the case in many markets and grocery stores around the world. This salad's simplicity makes it a favorite at STREETS Restaurant Café because of its fresh, clean and delicious flavors.

ingredients

tomato, 2 medium sized
cucumber, 4 oz/120 g
carrot, julienned, 4 oz/120 g
lettuce, 12 oz/375 g

vinaigrette

vinegar, 5 tablespoons
olive oil, 5 tablespoons
garlic, finely chopped, 1 tablespoon
salt. ½ teaspoon
pepper, ½ teaspoon
sugar, ½ teaspoon

Thinly slice tomato and cucumber into baton shapes and mix with carrot. Put vinaigrette ingredients in a screw-top jar and shake well. Add vinaigrette to vegetables and serve on bed of lettuce leaves.

Hot and Sour Fish Soup
Canh Chua Cá

This is a Vietnamese classic, particularly in the central coastal region of Vietnam, known for its abundance of seafood dishes. Along with being spicy, this soup also has sweet, sour, bitter and salty notes that combine for a well-balanced, tasty meal. Serves four.

ingredients

mackerel fillets, or similar fish, 7 oz/200 g

fish stock, 6 cups

chili oil, 2 teaspoons

garlic, chopped, 1 tablespoon

salt and pepper to taste

sugar, 1 tablespoon

pineapple, diced, 3½ oz/100 g

tamarind paste, 8 tablespoons

tomato, quartered, 1

spring onion, chopped, 1 tablespoon

fresh mint leaves, 1½ oz/40 g

okra, sliced, 1½ oz/40 g

taro, small dice, 1½ oz/40 g

nuoc mam (fish sauce), 2 tablespoons

red chili, finely sliced, 1

In a large saucepan, add chili oil and lightly brown garlic. Add fish stock. When starting to simmer, season with salt, pepper, sugar and tamarind paste. Add fish fillets, pineapple and tomato. Bring to simmer, add bean sprouts, spring onion, most of the mint, okra and taro. (Potato can be substituted if taro not available.) Remove from heat as soon as vegetables soften. Add fish sauce. Sprinkle red chili slices and remainder of fresh mint on top. Accompany with a bowl of steamed rice.

Pumpkin Soup
Súp Bí Đỏ

The Vietnamese pumpkin used in this dish differs from the large, orange North American pumpkin associated with Halloween and Thanksgiving. Vietnamese pumpkin is known in other many places as yellow or orange winter squash. However, any pumpkin, squash or gourd with orange flesh can be used for this soup. STREETS Restaurant Café serves this colorful soup with a surprise White Rose Dumpling nestled at the bottom of each bowl. Serves four.

ingredients

pumpkin, peeled and roughly diced, 13 oz/400 g
butter, 2½ oz/80 g
onion, roughly chopped, 3 tablespoons
carrot, roughly chopped, 2 tablespoons
ginger, roughly chopped, 1½ tablespoons
water, 6 cups
cream, ½ cup
White Rose Dumplings, 4 pieces (optional/see page 44)
honey, 4 teaspoons
salt and pepper to taste

Melt butter and brown onion. Add pumpkin, carrot and ginger and cover with water. Cook until vegetables are soft. Allow to cool, then blend with food processor until smooth. Reheat, add honey and season with salt to taste. Garnish with a swirl of cream and optional White Rose Dumplings.

Leafy Vegetable Soup with Rice Bowl
Canh Rau

This simple soup can be made with any seasonal leafy vegetables. The leaves of vegetables, roots and other produce – often discarded in many western households – are smartly used in inventive Vietnamese cooking. Serves four.

ingredients

ginger, 1 oz/20 g

vegetable stock, 6 cups

salt, to taste

black pepper, 1½ teaspoon

oyster sauce, 2 teaspoon

mustard leaves, 1½ oz/40 g

straw mushrooms, 1½ oz/40 g

wood ear mushrooms, soaked, julienned, 1 oz/20 g

carrot, julienned, 1½ oz/40 g

white cabbage, julienned, 1½ oz/40 g

soy sauce, 2 teaspoon

silken tofu, 16 small cubes

Add ginger to vegetable stock and bring to boil. Season to taste with salt, pepper and oyster sauce. Add mustard leaves, mushrooms, carrot and white cabbage. Return to boil and add soy sauce. Ladle into serving bowls. Garnish with tofu cubes and serve. Serve with steamed rice.

Winter Melon Soup with Shrimp
Canh Bí Đao Tôm

This is a basic, but delicious, soup that made its way on to the STREETS Restaurant Café menu after Trainees prepared it for staff members during a "family meal" at their dormitory. It was noted for being simple, clean and delicious. Serves four.

ingredients

winter melon, peeled, chopped, 4 oz/120 g

river shrimp, peeled and minced, 3 oz/90 g

red onion, chopped, 1 teaspoon

garlic, chopped, 1 teaspoon

salt, 1 teaspoon

vegetable stock, 4 cups

basil, fresh, 4 leaves

spring onion, chopped, 1 teaspoon

black pepper, 1 teaspoon

Gently boil winter melon a few minutes until it starts to soften. Marinate minced shrimp with red onion, garlic and salt. In saucepan, stir-fry shrimp until golden, add vegetable stock and winter melon. Bring stock to a simmer and season with salt and pepper to taste. Garnish with fresh basil, spring onion and black pepper. Serve with steamed rice.

BBQ Pork Baguette with Pate
Bánh Mì Thịt

The French are credited with introducing the baguette to Vietnam. The Vietnamese version is lighter with a crispier crust. It is the staple ingredient for the classic banh mi sandwich, sold in countless varieties throughout the country for breakfast, lunch and dinner. Common fillings include pâté, sliced meat, vegetables, soy sauce and chili sauce. Serves four.

ingredients

baguettes, 4
pork char siu, sliced (see recipe on page 74)
bbq sauce, any commercial brand, 1 tablespoon
black pepper, 1 teaspoon
pork liver pâté
lettuce, 1½ oz/ 40 g
mixed fresh herbs, 1½ oz/40 g
cucumber, 8 slices
soy sauce, 2 tablespoons

pork liver pâté

pork liver, sliced, 1½ lb/750 g
pork belly, minced, 8 oz/250 g
eggs, 2
milk, fresh, ¾ cup
baguettes, chopped, 2
butter, 2 tablespoons
salt, ½ teaspoon
pepper, ½ teaspoon
cinnamon powder, ½ teaspoon
vodka, 1½ tablespoons

For pork liver pâté: Place all ingredients except the butter in a food processor and blend until smooth. Line a brownie pan with aluminium foil and coat well with butter. Press mixture firmly into pan. Steam for 40 minutes then bake at 250 degrees for another 30 minutes. Allow to cool well before removing from pan. For baguette: Coat pork with bbq sauce and pepper, grill for five minutes. Slice warmed baguette lengthwise, spread on pâté, then add grilled pork, lettuce, fresh herbs and cucumber. Add a dash of soy sauce to the bread. Cut baguette in half and garnish with coleslaw.

Chicken Salad Baguette
Bánh Mì Gà

 A delicious, light meal that showcases Vietnamese mint, this STREETS Restaurant Café variation of the Vietnamese banh mi sandwich is a popular item at catered picnics and lunches prepared by the restaurant. Serves four.

ingredients

baguettes, 4

chicken breast, cooked and shredded, 13 oz/400 g

lime juice, 5 tablespoons

onion, chopped, 6½ oz/200 g

Vietnamese mint, chopped, 2 oz/60 g

shallot oil, 2½ tablespoons (fry chopped shallots
in oil until brown then remove shallots and use oil)

salt, 1 teaspoon

pepper, 1 teaspoon

butter, 3½ oz/100g

lettuce, 8 leaves

Mix together chicken, lime juice, onion, mint, shallot oil, salt and pepper. Split baguette lengthwise and warm in oven. Butter the bread well and fill with chicken salad and two lettuce leaves. To serve, slice in half and garnish with coleslaw.

Omelette Baguette
Bánh Mì Trứng

This sandwich is eaten for breakfast, lunch and dinner in Vietnam. The crisp, warm bread, scrambled eggs and fresh vegetables make for a filling sandwich. The thick, jam-like Hoi An chili sauce used in this sandwich is a specialty of the ancient town. Substitute with commonly available Thai-style hot sauce (such as Sriracha) and Thai sweet chili sauce (such as Mae Ploy.) Serves four.

ingredients

baguettes, 4

eggs, 4

milk, fresh, 2½ tablespoons

salt, 1 teaspoon

pepper, 1 teaspoon

shallot oil, 2 tablespoons (fry chopped shallots in oil until brown then remove shallots and use oil)

soy sauce, 2 tablespoons

Hoi An chili sauce, 2 tablespoons

tomato, 2 medium, sliced

lettuce, 8 leaves

In a bowl, beat the eggs with milk, salt and pepper. Heat shallot oil in omelette pan, pour in egg mixture and allow to set over medium heat, lifting the edges and tilting the pan occasionally to allow the uncooked egg to run underneath. When almost set, turn omelette over to cook other side. Remove from heat and allow to cool slightly. Slice into four pieces. Warm the baguettes, slice open and spread with soy sauce and Hoi An chili sauce or substitute. Add omelette slices. To serve, cut baguette in half and accompany with tomato and lettuce salad.

soups & baguettes

Hoi An Specialty Noodles with Pork
Cao Lâu

The most famous dish of Hoi An, Cao Lau is a must-eat on any visit. The slightly smoky, chewy noodles cannot be found outside the ancient city and reflect the historical influence of the Japanese in Hoi An. The recipe is thought to be more than 100 years old and delivers the quintessential taste of Hoi An with a delightful combination of color, texture, flavor and spice. STREETS Restaurant Café makes a vegetarian version by replacing the pork char siu with grilled tofu and a fresh tomato sauce. Substitute Japanese soba or udon noodles when making at home. Serves four.

ingredients

Cao Lau (substitute soba or udon noodles) 28 oz/800 g

bean sprouts, 7 oz/200 g

crispy wonton, 4 oz/120 g

pork char siu, (see below), 10½ oz/300 g

mixed herbs, basil, mint, cilantro, lettuce, 5½ oz/ 160

chili, sliced, 2 pieces garnish per serving

lime, wedge cut, 1 piece garnish per serving

Hoi An chili sauce (see substitute on page 5 or 20)

char siu

pork shoulder, 35 oz/1 kg

lemongrass, chopped, 3½ oz/100 g

soy sauce, 1 liter

five-spice powder, 1 tablespoon

sugar, 3½ oz/100 g

chili powder, 1 tablespoon

cornflour or cornstarch, 2 tablespoons

garlic, chopped, 2 tablespoons

shallots, chopped, 2 tablespoons

vegetable oil, 2½ tablespoons

pork stock, 1½ cups

cao lau sauce

shallot, chopped, 1 tablespoon

garlic, finely chopped, 1 tablespoon

lemongrass, chopped, 1 tablespoon

soy sauce, 1 cup

oyster sauce, 1/2 cup

five-spice powder, 1/2 teaspoon

sugar, 1 tablespoon

chili powder, 1 tablespoon

black pepper, 1 tablespoon

pork stock, 2 cups

The sweet and savory Char Siu is used in Cao Lau and Banh Mi Thit (page 68). Pork Char Siu comes from the Chinese and is popular in restaurants around the world. A sharp cleaver is best to thinly slice the meat.

For Char Siu

Cut pork into four pieces. In a large bowl, mix lemongrass, soy sauce, five-spice powder, sugar, chili powder, cornflour/cornstarch, garlic and shallots. Add pork and massage sauce thoroughly into meat. Marinate for at least one hour. Heat oil in wide pan and fry pork until brown. Add marinade and pork stock and simmer about 10 minutes or until brown. Allow meat to cool for 15 minutes before slicing thinly.

For Cao Lau

Sauté shallot, garlic and lemongrass in a teaspoon of oil. Add soy sauce, oyster sauce, five-spice powder, sugar, chili powder, pepper and pork stock and simmer gently for 10 minutes.

Bring pot of water to boil and lower noodles in using a strainer or sieve for about 20 seconds. Lift strainer, drain noodles and add to four deep serving bowls. Add bean sprouts to boiling water for 10 seconds, scoop out and add to noodles. Put mixed greens on one side of the bowl with slices of pork char siu on top of noodles. Top noodles with Cao Lau sauce, garnish with sliced chilis and crispy wonton. Accompany with small bowl of Hoi An chili sauce, or substitute, and lime wedges.

Cold Rice Noodle with Grilled Chicken and Herbs
Bún Gà Nướng

The bun noodle comes in many varieties that vary from region to region. Bun and most other Vietnamese noodles are made with rice flour. Prepared fresh daily, these noodles are extruded using hand-cranked machines and piled high at Vietnamese markets. Although more common in soups, bun noodles also are a delicious base for many cold salad-like dishes. Serves four.

ingredients

bun/rice noodles, 28 oz/800 g

chicken fillet, sliced diagonally, 8½ oz/240 g

bbq sauce, any commercial brand, 6 tablespoons

lettuce leaves, 4½ oz/120 g

mixed herbs (cilantro, basil, mint), 3½ oz/100 g

papaya and carrot pickle, 3 oz/ 80 g

peanuts, 1½ oz/40 g

fried shallots, 1½ oz/40 g

Vietnamese sweet and sour fish sauce

nuoc mam (fish sauce), ¼ cup

sugar, ½ cup

fresh-squeezed lemon juice, ½ cup

garlic, 2 cloves, minced

red chilis, 2, minced

Marinate chicken slices in bbq sauce for at least 10 minutes. Grill until medium. Slice thinly and diagonally. Quickly cook noodles in boiling water by placing in a sieve and lowering into the pot. This allows for easy removal and draining. Cook noodles in four batches. Put noodles into four individual serving bowls with lettuce, mixed herbs, papaya and carrot pickle, and grilled chicken. These ingredients are not mixed through the noodles to serve, but rather are arranged artfully on top of each dish. Garnish with peanuts and fried shallots. Accompany with Vietnamese sweet and sour fish sauce in separate bowls for each serving.

Beef Curry
Cà Ri Bò

Unlike more familiar Southeast Asian curries, this Vietnamese classic does not use coconut milk. This mild curry dish typically is enjoyed with a baguette to soak up the fragrant sauce. Serves four.

ingredients

lean beef, diced, 17 oz/500 g
garlic, minced, 8 cloves
lemongrass, minced, 8 stalks
shallots, minced, 2
Asian beef stock powder with curry, 2 tablespoons
five-spice powder, 4 tablespoons
nuoc mam (fish sauce), 4 teaspoons
pepper, 2 teaspoons
vegetable oil, 3 tablespoons
taro, peeled and diced, 17 oz/500 g
potato, peeled and diced, 17 oz/500 g
carrot, diced, 17 oz/500 g
beef stock, 4 cups
sugar, 1 tablespoon
baguettes, 4

Marinate beef for 15 minutes in mixture of garlic, lemongrass, shallot, Asian beef stock, five-spice powder, fish sauce and pepper. Pan fry taro, potato and carrot in oil until cooked. Remove from pan. Add more oil to pan and bring to high heat. Sauté beef for about three minutes, then add beef stock and sugar. Bring to a boil, then reduce to a simmer until beef is tender. Add cooked vegetables. Serve with baguette for dipping.

Chicken Rice
Cớm Gà

This is a very popular street food dish served throughout Vietnam. Three essential components to this dish include: yellow long-grain rice colored and flavored with turmeric, shredded chicken with mint and onion, accompanied by a simple, clear broth soup. Locally, the soup is poured over the rice to add flavour, and the liquid is thought to aid digestion. Serves four.

ingredients

chicken breast, 14 oz/400 g
onion, finely sliced, 4½ oz/120 g
Vietnamese mint leaves, 3½ oz/100 g
salt and pepper to taste
chicken stock powder, 1 teaspoon
lemon, quartered, 2
jasmine rice, 2 cups
turmeric powder, 1½ tablespoons
vegetable oil, 2 tablespoons
garlic, minced, 1½ tablespoons
water, 2 cups
chicken stock, 2 cups
carrot, julienned, 1½ oz/40 g
white cabbage, finely sliced, 2½ oz/60 g

Place chicken in saucepan, cover with water, and add pinch of salt. Bring to boil, then remove from heat, and allow chicken to continue cooking as the water cools. Set aside and retain stock. Allow cooked chicken to cool, and shred for salad. Add onion and mint leaves to the chicken then season to taste with salt, pepper, some chicken stock powder and juice from one lemon. Mix well.

For yellow rice: Heat oil in saucepan. Brown garlic. Stir in turmeric powder and rice, sauté for one minute then add two cups of water and one cup of chicken stock. Cover with lid. Turn to lowest heat. Cook very gently for about 20 minutes or until all liquid has been absorbed and rice is cooked. This absorption method ensures all the flavor of the stock is retained. In another pot, heat the remaining chicken stock, adding carrot and cabbage, season with chicken stock powder, salt and pepper to taste.

Divide rice between four plates, place scoop of chicken salad on one side, and garnish with a lemon wedge. Accompany with a small bowl of chicken stock.

Vietnamese Fried Rice with Seafood, Pork or Vegetables
Cơm Chiên Hải Sản, Thịt Heo hoặc Rau Củ

Vietnamese fried rice differs from its more common Chinese counterpart because of the lack of soy sauce. The resulting color of the rice should be off-white, not brown. This Vietnamese version of fried rice allows the flavors of the meat, vegetables and eggs to really shine. Serves four.

ingredients

seafood, shrimp, squid, fish fillets, finely chopped, 10½ oz/300 g

pork, minced, 10½ oz/300 g

mixed vegetables, carrot, green beans, finely chopped, 6½ oz/200 g

garlic, finely chopped, 1 tablespoon

black pepper, 1 teaspoon

salt, ¼ teaspoon

steamed rice, cooked and chilled 16 oz/500 g

eggs, beaten, 3

soy sauce, 2 tablespoons

shallots, 2 tablespoons

spring onion, finely chopped, 2 tablespoons

cucumber, 12 slices

tomato, 12 slices

vegetable oil, 4 tablespoons

onion, finely chopped, 2 tablespoons

soy sauce, 2 tablespoons (to taste)

Marinate pork or seafood with garlic, black pepper and salt for 10 minutes. Sauté until golden, set aside. Heat a large wok, then add vegetable oil. Stir fry onion, then add chopped vegetables if making a vegetable-fried rice. Move quickly while cooking with wok. Add rice and beaten eggs. Stir thoroughly for about one minute. Add pork or seafood or mixed vegetables to the rice mixture when the egg has cooked. Season to taste with a dash of soy sauce. Garnish with shallot and spring onion. Plate with sliced cucumber and tomato. Serves four.

Hand-Cut Rice Noodles with Pork, Shrimp and Quail Eggs
Mỳ Quảng

My Quang is the specialty noodle of Quang Nam Province in central Vietnam. "My" refers to the noodle and "Quang" the province. Among the ingredients that characterize the dish are quail eggs. These are considered a delicacy in many places but are sold in small, plastic-wrapped packages on the street and beaches in Vietnam as an inexpensive snack. My Quang noodles are hand-cut and rustic in appearance, and therefore not often served at restaurants catering to foreign travellers. However, My Quang is one of the most popular dishes served at STREETS Restaurant Café.

ingredients

quang noodles (substitute with flat-cut rice noodle)
28 oz/800 g
quail eggs, 8
chili oil, 2 tablespoons
pork loin, sliced, 8½ oz/240 g
shrimp, peeled, 7 oz/200 g
red onion, chopped, 1 tablespoon
garlic, chopped, 1 tablespoon
nuoc mam fish sauce, 1 tablespoon
black pepper 1/2 teaspoon
pork stock, 4 cups
vegetable oil, 2 tablespoons
peanuts, fresh, finely chopped, 1 tablespoon
chicken eggs, 1
seasoning powder, 1 tablespoon
sugar, 1 teaspoon
mixed fresh herbs and lettuce, 5½ oz/160 g
bean sprouts, 7 oz/200 g
tomato, 1/2 medium size

chili powder, 1 teaspoon
chili, sliced, 2 pieces garnish per serving
spring onion, chopped, 1 tablespoon
lemon, wedge cut, 1 piece garnish per serving
Hoi An chili sauce (see substitute on page 46)

Boil quail eggs, peel and sauté quickly in chili oil. Marinate pork and shrimp with red onion, garlic, fish sauce, sugar, seasoning powder, chili powder and black pepper for about 10 minutes. Sauté for three minutes with tomato, then add pork stock and chopped peanuts and bring to boil. Add raw eggs and cooked quail eggs. Gently stir until heated through. Season to taste with seasoning powder, salt and sugar. Cook noodles and divide among four bowls. Add fresh herbs, lettuce, and bean sprouts. Ladle stock over noodles. Garnish with spring onions, sliced chili, and lemon wedges. Serve with Hoi An chili sauce or substitute.

Caramelized Eggplant and Tofu Clay Pot
Cà Tím Kho Tộ

Clay pot dishes are common in Vietnam, with all the final cooking, preparation and serving done in one seasoned pot. The technique yields a delightful muddling of flavors. In this dish, the eggplant and tofu become infused with the sauce and carmelized with final cooking. The clay pot has a porous quality, and the overnight seasoning, as it soaks in lightly salted water, gives these dishes great flavor. Serves four.

ingredients

eggplant, diced, 28 oz/800 g
garlic, chopped, 1½ tablespoons
tofu, cubed, 4½ oz/120 g
vegetable oil for deep frying
spring onion, 4½ oz/120 g
red chili, finely slice, 2

clay pot sauce

oyster sauce, 2 tablespoons
dark soy sauce, 2 tablespoons
soy sauce, 2 tablespoons
sugar, 6 teaspoons
fish sauce, 2 tablespoons
black pepper, 1 teaspoon

Deep fry eggplant and drain well on paper towel. In a wok, sauté garlic until brown, add eggplant and stir-fry for one minute to absorb flavor. Mix all ingredients for clay pot sauce. Add this to wok along with tofu. Stir through gently. Carefully place in clay pot and bring to a gentle boil. Garnish with spring onion and sliced chili. Accompany with steamed rice.

Braised Pork Clay Pot with Quail Egg
Heo Kho Tộ

 The sauce in this dish is lighter than the eggplant and tofu clay pot dish. However, it has a rich flavor from the fatty pork shoulder, which becomes very tender during cooking. Heo Kho To, like My Quang, is topped with delicate, cooked quail eggs. Serves four.

ingredients

pork shoulder, cubed, 21 oz/ 600 g

quail eggs, boiled and peeled, 12

garlic, chopped, 1½ tablespoons

shallots, chopped, 1½ tablespoons

scallion, chopped, 4 tablespoons (garnish)

red chili, finely sliced, 1

onion, sliced, 1 tablespoon

lemongrass, chopped, 1 tablespoon

clay pot sauce

vegetable oil, 2 tablespoons

oyster sauce, 2 tablespoons

pork stock, 2 cups

dark soy sauce, 2 tablespoons

soy sauce, 2 tablespoons

sugar, 4 teaspoons

black pepper, 1 teaspoon

bbq sauce, 1 tablespoon

star anise, 2 pieces

In a wok, fry garlic, sliced onion and shallots until fragrant, then add pork cubes. Sauté for about five minutes. Add all clay pot sauce ingredients, and continue to sauté for another five minutes. Cover mixture with stock, bring to boil, then reduce to a simmer for about 20 minutes. Carefully place into individual clay pots, bring to a gentle boil, top with three quail eggs per bowl, and garnish with spring onions and red chili slices. Accompany with steamed rice.

Slow-Cooked Tuna Fillet Clay Pot
Cá Ngừ Kho Tộ

The key to this dish is using fresh tuna; we use Stripped Tuna, a local catch that fishermen call 'Cucumber Stripped,' from the East Sea. The steak-like texture of this dark, meaty fish allows it to hold up while cooking. The pineapple lightens the dish with a sour and sweet piquant. Serves four.

ingredients

tuna fillet, cubed, 21 oz/600 g

vegetable oil, 2 tablespoons

white wine, 2 tablespoons

garlic, chopped, 1 tablespoon

onion, sliced, 1 tablespoons

black pepper

spring onion

red chili, 8 fine slices

clay pot sauce

tomato, chopped, 8 tablespoons

pineapple, chopped, 4 tablespoons

fish sauce, 2 teaspoons

garlic, chopped, 6 cloves

shallots, chopped, 2 tablespoons

oyster sauce, 2 teaspoons

black pepper, 1 teaspoon

bbq sauce, any commercial brand, 2 tablespoons

Heat oil in wok, sauté fish cubes with white wine until lightly cooked. Remove from wok. Sauté garlic and onion until soft, then add pineapple, stir-frying until soft. Add all other clay pot sauce ingredients. Return fish to wok, folding in the sauce gently so it does not break up. Place in clay pot and heat through for 30 seconds on stove. Garnish with black pepper, spring onion and red chili slices. Accompany with steamed rice.

Sautéed Seasonal Vegetables
Rau Củ Quả Xào

Vegetables are a staple in Vietnam, where they grow in abundance. They are the staple of many dishes, preferred to the heavier meats typical of western cuisine. Try this recipe with any assortment of local vegetables in season. The key is to this dish is fresh vegetables and quick cooking to retain flavor. Use any six of the nine vegetables listed below to serve four.

ingredients

bok choy, 4½ oz/120 g

miniature/baby corn, 4½ oz/120 g

long beans, 4½ oz/120 g

zucchini, batons, 4½ oz/120 g

cauliflower, bite size florets, 4½ oz/120 g

broccoli, bite size florets, 4½ oz/120 g

red pepper, thin strips, 4½ oz/120 g

carrot, batons, 4½ oz/120 g

oyster or straw mushrooms, sliced, 4½ oz/120 g

vegetable oil, 2 tablespoons

garlic, sliced, 2 tablespoons

oyster sauce, 8 tablespoons

soy sauce, 6 tablespoons

sesame oil, 4 teaspoons

sugar, 2 teaspoons

salt and pepper to taste

fresh herbs such as mint, basil and coriander

Heat oil in wok and sauté garlic until brown. Add vegetables and stir-fry for approximately two minutes. Season with oyster sauce, soy sauce, sesame oil, sugar, salt and pepper to taste. Garnish each plate with fresh herbs and serve with steamed rice.

BBQ Pork Ribs
Sườn Heo Nướng

Women clad in farm boots with large, plastic buckets attached to their bicycles are a common sight in Hoi An. They are collecting food scraps from local restaurants in this daily routine, essential to traditional Vietnamese pig farming. Factory-farmed animals are less common in Vietnam, giving the local meat and poultry a freshness akin to organic meat and poultry found abroad. Serves four.

ingredients

pork ribs, cut along the bone, 42 oz/1.2 kg
bbq sauce, any commercial brand, 8 tablespoons
fried shallots, 1½ oz/40 g
green onion, sliced, 1½ oz/ 40 g

mango orange sauce

onion, chopped, 1 tablespoon

sugar, 2 tablespoons

orange juice, 3 tablespoons

mango jam, if unavailable use marmalade, peach or
apricot jam, 2 tablespoons

brown sugar, 2 tablespoons

salt and pepper mixed, 3 teaspoons

ketchup, 1 cup

Marinate pork ribs in bbq sauce for at least one hour. Wrap in foil and bake in the oven at 325°F (about 160°C) for an hour and 15 minutes. Mix together all sauce ingredients, open foil, spoon sauce over ribs, and broil an additional five minutes. Garnish with fried shallots and green onion. Serve with pickled vegetables and steamed rice.

Chicken Curry
Cà Ri Gà

This popular Vietnamese dish calls for the familiar coconut milk used in many Southeast Asian curries. This sweet element balances the sharpness of the lemongrass and the pungent curry powder. Serves four.

ingredients

chicken drumsticks, boneless, cut into pieces, 20 oz/560 g
vegetable oil for deep frying
salt and pepper to taste
turmeric powder, 2 teaspoons
garlic, chopped, 4 teaspoons
onion, chopped, 1 tablespoon
carrot, bite-size pieces, 2½ oz/60 g
zucchini, bite-size pieces, 2½ oz/60 g
eggplant, bite-size pieces, 1½ oz/40 g
lemongrass, finely chopped, 4 teaspoons
five-spice powder, 2 teaspoons
curry powder, 4 teaspoons
nuoc mam (fish sauce), 4 teaspoons
coconut milk, 1 cup
lemongrass stems, bruised, 1½ oz/40 g
basil leaves, ¼ cup
red chili, sliced, 1

Rub a mixture of salt, pepper and turmeric powder into chopped chicken pieces. Deep-fry chicken, then drain well on kitchen paper. In a clean wok, sauté garlic and onion in one tablespoon of oil. Then add carrot, zucchini, eggplant and lemongrass, and continue to stir fry until just cooked. Add five-spice powder, curry powder, nuoc mam fish sauce, coconut milk and some lemongrass stems to wok, and simmer for five minutes to heat ingredients. Ladle into individual bowls, and garnish with remaining lemongrass stems, basil leaves and red chili slices. Accompany with steamed rice.

Grilled Fish with Ginger Sauce
Cá Diêu Hồng Nướng Sốt Gừng

The combination of fresh ginger and white, mild fish is key to this dish. Tilapia, a mostly freshwater fish and favourite of chefs everywhere, is ideal and available in more than 100 species around the world. Tilapia are raised in farms and caught from rivers throughout Vietnam. Serves four.

ingredients

tilapia fillets, firm, 12 oz/320 g
salt and freshly ground pepper mix, 2 teaspoons
cornflour or cornstarch, 1 tablespoon
vegetable oil, 3 tablespoons
ginger sauce
garlic, minced, 2½ oz//60 g

ginger sauce

fish sauce, 3 tablespoons
salt and sugar mix, 1 tablespoon
ginger, minced,2½ oz/ 60 g
red chili, chopped,1½ oz/ 40 g
bbq sauce, any commercial sauce, 8 teaspoon

Rub salt and pepper mix into fish fillet and rest for 10 minutes. Dust underside of fillet only with cornflour or cornstarch. Pan fry until just cooked. Mix ginger sauce ingredients and spread thickly over each fish fillet. STREETS Restaurant Café serves this dish with bok choy and halved cherry tomatoes, browned with garlic, and a bowl of steamed rice.

Crispy Rice Pancake with Pork and Shrimp
Bánh Xèo

Banh Xeo is a classic dish thought to have originated in southern Vietnam but now popular throughout the country. The savory stuffed pancake is thin and crispy. It is wrapped in rice paper with mixed green herbs and eaten with the hands. Banh Xeo is typically cut into pieces with kitchen scissors at the table in Vietnamese restaurants, before being rolled by the diner. Serves four.

ingredients

filling

pork, thinly sliced tenderloin or shoulder,4½ oz/120 g

carrot, julienned, 4½ oz/120 g

bean sprouts, 4½ oz/120 g

black mushroom, julienned, 4½ oz/120 g

onion, thinly sliced, 4½ oz/120 g

shrimp, cooked and peeled, 4½ oz/120 g

vegetable oil, 8 tablespoons

marinade

oyster sauce, 4 tablespoons

fish sauce, 4 tablespoons

sugar, 2 tablespoons

chicken stock powder, 1 tablespoon

pancake batter

rice flour, 35 oz/1.25 kilos

spring onion, finely sliced, 4½ oz/120 g

turmeric powder, 4 teaspoons

water, 5 cups

dipping sauce

fresh soy beans, 1 oz/30 g

peanuts, 1 oz/30 g

sugar, ½ teaspoon

pork liver, 1½ oz/40 g

garlic, minced, 1 tablespoon

salt and pepper to taste

fish sauce to taste

water, 1½ tablespoons

mixed greens (basil, lettuce, cilantro)

rice paper, 20 pieces

For marinade and filling

Mix marinade ingredients in stainless steel or glass bowl, add pork strips and marinate for 15 minutes. Heat oil in wok, and fry onion until soft. Add garlic and continue frying until onion begins to brown. Add pork in small batches, cooking quickly on high heat until done. Assemble pork and other filling ingredients in individual bowls close to stove for easy access. A vegetarian option can replace the pork and shrimp with a medley of wood ear and straw mushrooms, finely sliced and quickly stir-fried with the onion and garlic.

For the pancake

Put dry ingredients in large bowl. Slowly add water while stirring well to form a thick batter. Add green onion and allow batter to rest for 30 minutes. In a small, shallow frypan heat one tablespoon of oil. Put one ladle into pan, tilting to cover the base with the batter. Place one tablespoon of each filling ingredient onto half of the pancake while it is cooking. When pancake has cooked through, fold other half over the filling and slide onto plate.

For the dipping sauce

Use a food processor to separately grind pork liver, soy beans and peanuts then mix together in bowl. Sauté garlic until fragrant, add pork liver mixture, and continue to sauté for about three minutes. Add water and cook for further 10 minutes. Allow to cool. Serve in individual bowls.

Presentation and eating

Cut rice paper into halves and put four to six pieces on each plate beside the pancake. Garnish with a handful of mixed greens. To eat, cut pancake into four or six slices. Place a slice onto a piece of rice paper and add some mixed greens. Roll and dip into sauce.

Baguette Bread Pudding with Passion Fruit Sauce
Bánh Pudding

Aside from fruit, desserts are not common at the end of Vietnamese meals, as a sweet element is integrated within most savory dishes. This dessert combines the ubiquitous baguette with one of the most lush and fragrant fruits in Vietnam to deliver a STREETS Restaurant Café original dish. Serves four.

ingredients

baguettes, thickly sliced, 3 medium or 1 long

coconut milk, 1¾ cups

milk, 2½ tablespoons

egg, 1

sugar, 2½ oz/70 g

salt, ¼ teaspoon

vanilla essence, ¼ teaspoon

butter, 1 oz/25 g

raisins, 2 oz/ 50 g

mango jam

mango, peeled and finely diced, 8 oz/250 g

sugar, 2 oz/50 g

passion fruit sauce

passion fruit, 16 oz/500 g

sugar, 2 oz/50 g

In large bowl, mix together coconut milk, fresh milk, egg, sugar, salt, vanilla essence and melted butter. Add bread, and stir through until well-coated and liquid has been absorbed. Line a large shallow baking pan with aluminium foil and coat well with melted butter. Place bread slices on the tray in a single layer, but packed closely together. Top with raisins. Bake at 350°F (175°C) for 45 minutes.

Meanwhile, make the mango jam by mixing in saucepan with sugar and simmering gently for 30 minutes. Stir frequently and watch that it does not burn.

Make the passion fruit sauce in another pan by mixing the juice from the passion fruit with the sugar and simmering gently for about 40 minutes, stirring frequently. Cut squares of bread pudding and top with mango jam and spoon over passion fruit sauce.

Coconut Ice Cream Parfait
with Pineapple Drizzle
Kem Dừa

This dessert is a basic but decadent combination of homemade pineapple sauce and grilled pineapple, atop coconut ice cream. The contrast of colors and textures are amazingly complementary. Use the best quality coconut ice cream available. Serves four.

ingredients
coconut ice cream
mint leaves for garnish

pineapple jam
pineapple, finely diced, 16 oz/500 g
sugar, 7 oz/ 200 g

pineapple sauce
pineapple juice, freshly pressed, 2 cups
sugar, 7 oz/ 200 g

grilled pineapple
pineapple, 1 quarter cut in wedge shapes
sugar, 2 teaspoons

For pineapple jam
Cook diced fresh pineapple and sugar in a small saucepan gently for 20 minutes, stirring frequently. Allow to cool.

For pineapple sauce
Put ingredients in small saucepan and simmer for 20 minutes.

For grilled pineapple
Coat wedges in sugar and grill on dry non-stick pan for one minute. To serve, put two scoops of ice cream in a parfait glass, drizzle about a tablespoon of pineapple jam, then pineapple sauce. Finally, garnish with fresh mint leaves and grilled pineapple.

Crème Flan with Vietnamese Coffee Glaze
Kem Flan

This STREETS Restaurant Café recipe takes the "kem flan" – a common gelatin-like street food – and elevates it with a rich, creamy consistency. It's topped with a sauce made from Vietnamese coffee beans. Serves four.

ingredients
eggs, 2
cream, 1/2 cup
milk, 3/4 cup
sugar, 5/8 cup
fresh mint leaf garnish, 4
Vietnamese drip coffee, ½ cup

Vietnamese coffee caramel sauce
Vietnamese drip coffee, ½ cup
sugar, 7/8 cup
water, 2 teaspoons

Heat oven to 300°F (150°C). In large bowl, lightly beat the eggs, then add cream, milk, drip coffee and sugar.

Make the Vietnamese coffee caramel sauce in a separate small sauce pan, mix ingredients, and simmer 45 minutes. Allow to cool.

Lightly cover the bottom of each ¾ cup oven-proof mold using approximately half of the Vietnamese coffee caramel sauce. Divide the mixed ingredients between individual molds, place in baking tin and add water until half way up the side of the molds. Put in oven for 30 to 40 minutes or until knife blade inserted emerges clean.

Refrigerate for two hours, then gently remove from molds. Drizzle remaining Vietnamese coffee caramel sauce over flan, and garnish with fresh mint leaves.

Coffee Frappé
Cà Phê Sữa Đá Pha Kem Béo

A drinkable dessert, this STREETS Restaurant Café beverage is a twist on the classic sweetened Vietnamese iced coffee. Serves four.

ingredients

Vietnamese coffee, 2 cups

sweetened condensed milk, 2 cups

fresh milk, 2 tablespoons

crushed ice

whipped cream

chocolate powder, 1 teaspoon

Pour cooled coffee, condensed milk, fresh milk and crushed ice into blender. Process until well-blended and thick. Divide among four large specialty drink glasses. Garnish with whipped cream and sprinkle with chocolate powder.

Vietnamese Coffee
Cà Phê Đá, Cà Phê Sữa Đá

Vietnamese coffee is drip-brewed. It is typically prepared in individual cups using small, aluminium filters known as phins. The phin sits atop the small glass in which the coffee is served. Inside is a chamber for the ground coffee and hot water. Below the main chamber is a slotted plate, which adds another layer of filtering. Boiling water is poured on top of the coffee in the main chamber. The brew is covered with a press plate and lid, and left to drip brew.

The result is a simple, but potent cup of coffee with a chicory, sometimes described as a "chocolatey" flavor. The filtering process is slow because of the dense packing of the coffee, making its consumption more of an event than a quick cup of energy on-the-go.

The French introduced coffee production and consumption to Vietnam, and elsewhere in Southeast Asia, in the mid-19th century. Despite its European influence, Vietnamese coffee has a taste of its own. Today, Vietnam is among the world's leading coffee producers.

The more traditional black coffee (ca phe da) is filtered into a cup hot. It can also be poured into a glass filled with a single large ice cube.

Iced coffee with milk (ca phe sua da) starts with the same individual filtered cup. In a seperate glass, sweetened condensed milk is added, followed by the ice, then the coffee. The "Saigon style" version is a milder brew served in a tall, slender glass with a long spoon to blend the drink together.

Dalat Sangria
Vang Đỏ Đà Lạt Pha Trái Cây Tươi

This is STREETS Restaurant Café's take on the popular Spanish sangria. It uses Vietnamese wine from the city of Dalat in the Central Highlands region of Vietnam, as well as fresh-squeezed local fruits. Like all sangria, it is best served on ice with fresh fruit. Serves four to six.

ingredients

Dalat red wine, (substitute any inexpensive, basic red wine) 750 ml bottle

Triple Sec, 245 ml

simple syrup, 135 ml (dissolve two parts sugar into one part boiling water, remove from heat)

freshly squeezed orange juice, 520 ml

freshly squeezed lime juice, 0.5 ml

dragon fruit, small cubes, 1 tablespoon

pineapple, small cubes, 1 tablespoon

asian pear, small cubes, 1 tablespoon

Combine Triple Sec, simple syrup, orange juice and lime juice in a small pitcher. Add wine, stir well and chill. Serve in specialty cocktail or large wine glasses, squeeze lime and pour over ice. Top the glass off with a teaspoon of the cubed fresh fruits.

Streetini Specialty Cocktail

This signature cocktail at STREETS Restaurant Café puts an international spin and Asian twist on the classic martini, incorporating Russian vodka, French cognac and Vietnamese ginger for a refreshing cocktail.

ingredients

fresh ginger juice, 40 ml
vodka (Stolichnaya), 40 ml
cognac (Remy Martin), 20 ml
simple syrup, 20 ml, (dissolve two parts sugar into
one part boiling water, remove from heat)
julienned ginger, 5 pcs
lime juice, 20 ml
small ice cubes, 3 pcs
sliced lemon, 1 wedge

To make ginger juice: Wash and peel ginger and put in blender. Strain mixture to yield juice.

Chill martini glass. Combine vodka, cognac, simple syrup, ginger juice and lime juice into a martini shaker with several small ice cubes. Shake well and strain into glass. Garnish with julienne ginger and thinly sliced lemon. Serves one.

For more information and to
support STREETS

www.streetsinternational.org

notes